Transformational Leadership:

92 Tips For Using The Different Types Of Leadership To Identify Leadership Traits That Uncover Your Leadership Strengths

By Gary Vurnum

www.92Tips.com and
www.Vurnum.com

Transformational Leadership: 92 Tips For
Using The Different Types Of Leadership
To Identify Leadership Traits That Uncover
Your Leadership Strengths
ISBN: 1450561454
EAN- 13: 9781450561457

For Katie, Skye, and Connor

"It's no secret that you'll never find a miserable lucky person. Perhaps that's a clue!"

"The Amazing Secret Behind THE Single Most Important Skill You Can Learn To Thrive In Your Job - No Matter What The Economy Is Doing!"

You will receive, completely free...

- Full access to the *"8 Steps Towards Becoming The Leader You Need To Be To Succeed"* video

- Full access to the audio mp3 recording

- Full access to the written transcript

- Full access to the implementation workbook

-Your own motivational screensaver

- PLUS a special gift worth up to $50!

Go to www.Leadership-Secrets.com/free

An important part of success in life is the ability to lead.

1

It is important that we not only be able to lead others but be willing to lead ourselves. No one succeeds in life by simply following others. Sometimes we simply must strike a bold new path for ourselves.

Being a good leader is more than simply being at the forefront of the crowd.

2

A leader must act. Too often we simply accept that someone looks or sounds like a leader and too rarely do we actually look at the actions that leader performs, and that is the true test of leadership.

Be alert to new opportunities.

3

Some might simply say that certain people are successful because they are lucky to be in the right place at the right time. Maybe so, but if they hadn't had their eyes open for the opportunity, then it wouldn't have mattered if they were in the right place.

Accept inspiration from wherever it comes; even your opponents.

4

The wisest leaders constantly study their competition. In war, politics, and business we constantly see examples of this research and reconnaissance. Too many times many concentrate on finding a weakness to exploit. If you want to be a leader of positive change don't fall victim to this trend. Instead, if you find a weakness, make sure to avoid that pitfall yourself.

Learn something new and promote in new ways every day.

5

This means you must continually seek to expand your horizons, internally and externally. Feed your mind with new lessons and knowledge, but constantly expand your social horizons as well. Seek out and meet new people and immerse yourself in new social situations. You never know when these new experiences will help you in your leadership role.

Search for and find answers in subtle clues.

6

Look beneath the surface and constantly question. This means that you will need to step off the traditional paths of knowledge. Don't simply read books in the literary canon or the bestsellers list. Take seminars rather than classes as there is more room for questioning and debate. Seek out the unconventional thinkers, teachers, and writers.

Improvise if no existing solutions are available.

7

No excuses. Necessity is the mother of invention. How do you know it won't work if you've never tried it before? Remember, not all approaches need to come from the front. Look at your problem from all sides and systematically attempt different solutions in various combinations.

Make at least one person you care about happy every day.

8

If you make it a point to be thoughtful and caring for one person every day then soon this thoughtful, caring behavior will become a habit and that habit will spread to the others around you. Making someone else happy also feeds your own personal happiness. Just imagine how much better the world would be if we all did a little bit more to spread happiness.

Never let negativity be your last word on the subject.

9

If your final words are negative than no matter how hopeful you may be about the potential of a project or action the lasting impression you give to others is one of negativity. Accentuate the positive and you are more likely to see a positive outcome.

Leadership starts with humility.

10

To be a highly successful leader, you must first humble yourself like a little child and be willing to serve others. Nobody wants to follow someone who is arrogant. Be humble as a child, always curious, always hungry and thirsty for knowledge. For what is excellence but knowledge plus knowledge plus knowledge - always wanting to better yourself, always improving, always growing.

Regardless of how busy you are, always take time to do what you love doing.

11

Being an alive and vital person vitalizes others. When you are pursuing your passions, people around you cannot help but feel impassioned by your presence. This will make you a charismatic leader. Whatever it is that you enjoy doing, be it writing, painting, sports, reading, networking, or working on entrepreneurial ventures, set aside time every week, to pursue these activities.

Victory belongs to those who want it the most and stay in it the longest.

12

When you have a dream you're aiming for, make sure you take consistent action every day. I recommend doing at least five things every day that will move you closer to your dream.

Every time you break your word, you lose power.

13

Successful leaders keep their word and their promises. You can accumulate all the toys and riches in the world, but you only have one reputation in life. Your word is gold. Honor it.

Find yourself a mentor.

14

Preferably someone who has already achieved a high degree of success in your field. Don't be afraid to ask. You've got nothing to lose. In addition to mentors, take time to study autobiographies of great leaders that you admire. Learn everything you can from their lives and model some of their successful behaviors.

Develop your own leadership style.

15

History books are filled with leaders who are soft-spoken, introverted, and quiet, all the way to the other extreme of being out-spoken, extroverted, and loud, and everything in between. Be yourself, your best self, always competing against yourself and bettering yourself, and you will become a first rate YOU instead of a second rate somebody else.

Be a giver.

16

Leaders are givers. By giving, you activate a universal law as sound as gravity life gives to the giver, and takes from the taker. The more you give, the more you get. If you want more love, respect, support, and compassion, give love, give respect, give support, and give compassion. Be a mentor to others. Give back to your community.

Work with and utilize the strengths and working styles of the personalities in your team.

17

By correctly positioning the individual member strengths and compensating for weaknesses, as a leader, you can bring the team into a productive balance and harmony.

A leader should take full responsibility for a task.

18

He should do so, not just before he accepts to take it, but also after it has been accomplished. As much as he is responsible for his team's success, he should also be responsible for any failure. He represents the whole team so whatever happens to it, he is the one responsible.

Never make excuses and blame something or someone else for failed tasks.

19

What you should do, instead, is to accept the fact that something went wrong with the organization, even if it is not directly your fault. It is normal to make mistakes. In fact, mistakes are opportunities to learn something better. As a leader, he must ensure that the team members learn from these mistakes and that these errors will not be repeated next time.

Have full control of your own reactions.

20

You may not have full control over other people and are not expected to have full control over their actions, but you must have full control of your own! Knowing what to do over unexpected and unpredictable situations will make you responsible, hence giving you the feeling of power.

The key to being successful is to be around people who empower you to reach the next level!

21

In order to exceed your present reach, you need to be around people who will help you stretch a little farther. A sign of a very intelligent person is to be smart enough to realize that you need to learn from others who can contribute to your WHY in life.

Outside influences don't usually determine your happiness or success.

22

Rather it is how you react to those influences – good or bad. So how do you change your reactions to those outside forces? Make how you react a conscious priority, which means you need to practice daily.

Humor is vital.

23

When things aren't going your way, keep everything in perspective and relax. Positive self- confident feelings not only help you achieve more; they also make others want to be associated with you. People are drawn to others who have an upbeat outlook, who have a can- do attitude.

Constant complainers don't collect an easy following.

24

One of a leader's most important jobs is to set a positive and self- confident tone, exuding the attitude that failure is not an option. A positive attitude is the cornerstone of leadership. It's the same confidence that a quarterback, a golfer, or a tennis star projects every time they come out of the locker room.

Break the negative energy cycle —
if you see yourself spiraling down
or in a rut, mix it up!

25

When you see one of your team members in a rut of unproductive or unprofessional behavior address it, don't let it fester. Active listening takes time. Work at it, to hear what your team wants. Often just by being heard, problems can go away and people really make a big turnaround.

You must be the emotional manager of your office - not your assistant.

26

In a family, parents must be the emotional managers or chaos rules the home. In your business, you must wear that mantel, albeit reluctantly at times. It's part of your leadership role and power. Hone it, as well as your reactions to external events, and you'll see the culture around you shift to the positive.

When in doubt, don't hire – keep looking.

27

You can't grow revenues consistently faster than your ability to get enough of the right people to implement that growth and still become a great company. So unless candidates for the open position have that can-do attitude and are a strong fit for your company in who they are – don't hire them. The skills can be taught; the and-then-some positive attitude cannot.

A negative attitude will pull you down and with it your professional results.

28

A positive attitude will pull you over the rough spots and energize you to lift your results to new heights — to match your vision. Whether you need an attitude adjustment a couple of times a day, once a week or only occasionally, never forget that your attitude determines your altitude. Don't let outside people or events bring yours down.

The "no news is good news" approach to leading knowledge workers is a recipe for disaster.

29

You might think that if employees aren't screwing up, they don't need to hear from you. But knowledge workers want to be recognized. They need your attention. Recognize progress and give recognition to foster their talents and help them move in the right direction and fuels their enthusiasm. Avoid focusing only on what's wrong and acknowledge what's going right.

Job uncertainty and fear may prevent employees from speaking up about a change that's needed.

30

It's your job to notice when individuals lost interest, struggle in their current position, or slack off for some unknown reason. Address these issues head on instead of allowing them to continue.

There's no joy in just getting by.

31

You don't help employees by allowing a bad fit to continue. Tough love with self and others is part of moving into the new economy.

A wise leader helps individuals recognize problems and learn from problems.

32

Don't wait until there is a crisis to raise a touchy subject and give feedback. Regular feedback helps employees grow.

Your primary role as a leader is to help your team contribute their talents.

33

Involve them in key decisions and welcome their input. Encourage collaboration with others who will stretch their minds and capabilities. Make sure employee talents are visible, seen and appreciated by others in the organization.

We all have it in us to be a leader.

34

You need to be brave and determined to take control and remember that all you can do in life is to try your best. You are only sure about living one life, so just be happy and not accept second best. Be a leader in life, not a follower!

Any successful person you can think of will have a success team around them.

35

You too need to form your own success team in whatever venture you choose. Whether it is lawyers, accountants, advisors, mentors or experts, it is vital that you have this team around you.

You can't do everything yourself.

36

There is no way you can have the level of expertise you need to succeed in all the areas you need. By picking a team of advisors to help you and guide you, you give yourself the time to focus on your area of specialty.

If you fail to prepare, you are preparing to fail.

37

If one has truly prepared and something goes wrong the strength of the rest of what you've prepared for usually makes this something easier to handle without crisis and panic.

Most people don't fulfil their dreams because of their fear of success, not the fear of failure!

38

It's the fear of actually accomplishing what they set out to do. The fear of living life to the fullest may have paralyzed you. This will cause you to never really try in your business, or if you do try, to sabotage your efforts so you never have to face your fear of success.

Leadership is not about bullying and high-handedness or even intellectual or financial superiority.

39

It is about playing to strengths, working around or minimizing weaknesses, authenticity and not being fazed by challenges. Above all, it is about being straight in communications both internally and externally.

Have a "can-do" mentality and avoid disempowering language when addressing your team.

40

Words such as "I'll try to" or "I need you to..." and other indirect language undermine the communication: "trying" to do anything is preparing for failure, not taking personal responsibility for causing something to happen.

Make sure that you actively listen.

41

Watching facial expression and body language is often a far more accurate barometer than the words that are being used. Nice things being said where the smile doesn't reach the eyes is an obvious example. When we are actively listened to we feel valued and are far more likely to engage in negotiation and compromise - so it is essential that you try to actively listen whenever possible.

Be careful of the tone of your voice when you respond or ask questions.

42

It is all too easy to come across as judgmental or as an interrogator from the Spanish Inquisition.

Use empathy.

43

Acknowledge difficulties, but be careful not to fall into the trap of going into anecdotes from your experience. "I sense that you are finding this rather difficult" rather than "Oh I know, it happened to me but mine was bigger, more difficult etc"

Take a real interest.

44

If you are simply going through the motions the lack of sincerity will be obvious to others. Leave your ego behind, concentrate on the other person.

No longer does a one size fits all leadership model really work.

45

We can't treat everyone the same and expect that everything will just "work out" somehow. Managers and leaders must have a framework with which to manage their workers in a way that honors everyone's unique and specific position on the job.

When you seek to empower your team, you will gain their loyalty.

46

Workers want to give their supervisor their best when they are listened to and respected. Without fear, their minds can be creative and innovative. When managers are willing to accommodate special requests and it doesn't interfere with product or service delivery, then their employees will be sure to give back their best in return. Giving away power only increases a manager's power.

Don't be a total pushover and only do what employees want!

47

As a manager, you have a two- fold job—you are to represent your employees' desires, opinions and suggestions to management while at the same time communicating management's issues, concerns and expectations to your employees. This is not an easy line to walk.

You will never get the best from your employees if they don't respect you.

48

You cannot be a doormat for your employees to walk over. If they believe you have no bottom line or nonnegotiables, then they will never be satisfied and always asking for more. You will feel used and abused and the truth is, you asked for it.

As a manager, you must set the bar high.

49

Expect great things from each and every one of your workers. If you only expect mediocrity, mediocrity is exactly what you will get. Set the standards and lead by example. If your workers see you giving it your all, it will be difficult for them to perform below standard.

If you see something that needs to be done and know you can make it happen, just get started!

50

A leader sees opportunity and captures it. A leader sees a future that can be different and better, and helps others see that picture too. A leader knows they can't do it alone. A leader is a coach. A leader is an encourager. A leader views change as their ally. A leader is willing to take risks today for something better tomorrow. A leader is a learner.

There is no single small skill set that defines the perfect leader or guarantees success.

51

Everyone is born with a unique set of natural abilities. And all of us can develop skills and styles to complement those natural abilities.

We were all born to lead, in our own way.

52

We may not be the Chairman of the Board. We may not be the person on the stage. We may not lead with oratory or flair. We may lead by compassion. We may lead by example. We all can lead. We all have the ability to be remarkable leaders.

Leadership isn't about position.

53

Leadership isn't about power. Leadership is about potential — your potential. You are a leader. Claim and believe this to be true, for it is. Stake your claim and make a difference in the world around you.

Good rapport lies at the heart of your effective communication.

54

It enables you to get people's attention and for them to take onboard what you have to say. Good rapport comes from body language and how you say things through the tonality and rhythm of your voice. Together, body language and how you say your words make up 93% of your communication. What you say is only 7%!

How you hold and use your body makes up 55% of your communication.

55

Use your body to match people's body movements. There will be a certain pattern and rhythm to their movements that you can copy. It's wise to pay attention to this even if you have good intentions for doing otherwise. You could easily be misinterpreted.

Voice tonality and rhythm is 38% of your communication.

56

The tone of your voice and the pace that you talk affects the message that you are trying to portray. People use different tones and speeds when talking. Do your best to adjust your voice to come closer to their way of talking.

Leadership is about behavior first, skills second.

57

Good leaders are followed chiefly because people trust and respect them, rather than the skills they possess. Leadership is different to management. Management relies more on planning, organizational and communications skills.

If you truly want to be a leader, you CAN develop leadership ability!

58

Leadership relies on qualities such as integrity, honesty, humility, courage, commitment, sincerity, passion, confidence, positivity, wisdom, determination, compassion and sensitivity - which all can be learned!

Leadership is about finding the best in yourself and giving the best of yourself.

59

Great leaders always go first, setting the example, walking the talk, doing not dabbling. Isn't it time that you act in the same way?

Leadership matters.

60

Any one person may have an effect on the behavior of others at any time. The nature and intent of that effect determines the influence, direction and outcome of leadership. Organizations depend on leadership for direction, momentum and a plan for sustainable success.

Never be reluctant to admit that you don't know.

61

There is no one who knows everything. So if you don't know much about leadership, all that has to be done is to read up on it!

People want leaders who treat them with genuine compassion, courtesy, and respect.

62

They want leaders who help them become more successful. They want leaders who inspire them with a vision for a better world and show them how to go there.

Delegate jobs to the people who can get it done.

63

This doesn't mean that person has all the skills for execution, but that they are able to martial the right resources. Sometimes the first step in the project will be education. Maybe your delegate has to attend a seminar or take a course to get up to speed.

Always begin with clearly defined goals and then prepare plans for achieving them.

64

Effective leaders have the courage to set a direction and then make changes as new information becomes available. They communicate with candor knowing that people perform at their best when they know what is expected.

Pay attention to what people say during a meeting.

65

Do their ideas contribute toward achieving the objective of the meeting? If so, this shows that they're working as part of a team to help find solutions. Do their ideas build upon what others just said? If so, this shows that they're paying attention to the dialogue. Do their ideas demonstrate originality, creativity, and knowledge? If so, this shows they're working hard to add value.

Evaluate the comments and behavior during a meeting.

66

Are the participants working to support each other? Are people contributing to the safe environment that is essential for open creative thinking? Are people adding high-value contributions (instead of stories or jokes that distract everyone)? Note that chronic unproductive behavior betrays either fear, a lack of effective work skills, or misunderstood expectations.

Leadership involves more than watching people talk.

67

Thus, observe the dynamics of the meeting process. Is the chairperson leading everybody through methodical steps that take them to a result? Is the meeting being conducted in such a way that the participants feel that it is a fair process? Is the chairperson helping others perform at their best so that the group can produce an outstanding result?

Do not occupy yourself with things that do not concern you.

68

If you habitually engage in something you hardly know anything about, you are making your situation far worse than the one who does nothing at all. On the other hand, some people seem to get satisfaction by intervening in other people's business. Always be alert and possess utmost care to ensure that no one meddles in your own affairs.

Decide first whether a task is worth your precious time.

69

Just a simple thought: If it will just eat your time away from the more important things you consider in your life, then it's not worth your time. Period.

Avoid incurring obligations beyond your capacity.

70

Instead, nurture your skills and abilities for the time being. There will come a right time for you to step up; and when that perfect moment arrives, waste no opportunity. But as long as you are not sure of the outcome, say "no" for the meantime especially if the favor will just derail your strategy.

If you have to think, take a break and take your time.

71

Matters that can cause an adverse change in your life require a lot of thinking. There are times when people act on first impulse, on what they feel and think at that very instant. Certainly, this is not always the case.

If you do nothing differently then nothing will change.

72

In order for anything to be possible you have to take action. Secondly you have to start by looking at yourself rather than blaming your position on others. Be honest with yourself. Close your eyes, see yourself at work as others see you.

Identify your goals and when you want to achieve them by.

73

Make your goals realistic but challenging. Work out a daily programme to achieve your goals. Talk about them to others, make them real and make them happen. Remember to celebrate your achievements. If things go wrong remember that it happens to successful people too.

Make sure you model promotion worthy behaviors.

74

It may help you if you think about those people you know who are good role models, or about what makes the ideal boss? Think about what makes them good. Make a list of their attributes. In house promotion or a job elsewhere either way you will need a reference so the opinion of those you currently work for will count.

Listen to feedback with an open mind.

75

Ask for support and training in the areas where development is needed. Show your boss your plan of action and involve them in the process. Be honest in your dealings with yourself and others. Know your strengths and face your weaknesses. Believe in yourself and others will believe in you.

Set challenging but realistic targets.

76

Aim high. Communicate your vision, and keep doing so. Ensure that all stake holders understand and subscribe to the same vision.

Celebrate success!

77

Remember to thank people for their contribution, give credit where it due and be generous with it. Develop professional honesty within your staff, constructive feedback can be invaluable.

What is your dream?

78

What are your goals for the
future? What do you want to
achieve in your life in the next
week? Month? Year? Five years?
What would you like people to
remember you for after you have
left this world? Think big -
challenge yourself.

Think about the language you use.

79

Sound positive, if others think you are confident it can be achieved they will gain confidence too. Develop a "can do" mentality within your staff. For every problem there is a solution, encourage others to see themselves as problem solvers not problem givers.

Discover your personality traits and how they relate to leadership.

80

When we know ourselves, we can maximize our positive traits, and become aware of our weaker areas, which help us to achieve our leadership potential.

Hone your communication skills.

81

These are not limited to your public speaking skills either. This includes your writing style and your body language. Your ability to communicate effectively enhances your ability to improve interpersonal relationships.

Learn how to learn.

82

Examine different teaching methods and learning styles to identify how you and those you may lead learn best. This skill will greatly enhance your ability to make decisions and give clear instructions.

Never once did a leader become a great leader by being pessimistic and negative.

83

Never has anything been accomplished of value by looking at a problem and complaining without offering a solution to the problem. In fact, a leader who only offers a negative picture remains a leader for a short time, a time when they are noticed but become irrelevant.

To be effective, you have to give the people who follow you hope of better things.

84

In doing so, you will rise to higher levels and accomplishes great things. When you lose sight of the lofty challenge of being a positive visionary in any organization, as a leader, you will be destined to fail, for no one will follow a leader who is going over a cliff.

You can choose to be whoever you wish to be.

85

You can look at challenges and problems and offer real solutions and visions for the future that people can grasp onto, or you can see the problem and rub everyone's nose in it as you complain about it until no one is listening anymore.

Review the direction you are heading as a leader.

86

Review the choices before you and make the best one, based not on comfort or habit, but based on the future result you desire.

Aspiring leaders need to be true to themselves; not slavishly following other's ideas.

87

Leadership is all about being yourself and demonstrating authenticity rather than learning some text book formula. Role models can be powerful and it doesn't hurt to model excellence when found; executive coaching is based on this premise.

Reveal your weaknesses, and let others know you are not super- human!

88

Obviously this doesn't mean technical weaknesses or functional failings; this would fatally flaw your performance! Just reveal your personality quirks - and just make the most of being you - whoever that may be!

Rely on your ability to read situations.

89

Develop a 'feel' for an environment, and interpret soft data without having to be told. Understand when team morale is patchy or when complacency needs shaking up.

Continually learn about the motives, attributes and skills of your important subordinates.

90

Get to know your people through formal and, often better, informal contact such as when travelling together.

Make sure you tell people what's important.

91

You should have crafted your one or two simple messages about your mission and your people's part in achieving it. Show up a lot and you get more opportunities to share those messages.

If you want to be larger than life, you need a dream that's larger than life.

92

Small dreams won't serve you or anyone else. It takes the same amount of time to dream small than it does to dream big. So be Big and be Bold! Write down your One Biggest Dream. The one that excites you the most. Remember, don't be small and realistic; be bold and unrealistic! Go for the Gold, the Pulitzer, the Nobel, the Oscar, the highest you can possibly achieve in your field.

"The Amazing Secret Behind THE Single Most Important Skill You Can Learn To Thrive In Your Job - No Matter What The Economy Is Doing!"

You will receive, completely free...

- Full access to the *"8 Steps Towards Becoming The Leader You Need To Be To Succeed"* video

- Full access to the audio mp3 recording

- Full access to the written transcript

- Full access to the implementation workbook

-Your own motivational screensaver

- PLUS a special gift worth up to $50!

Go to www.Leadership-Secrets.com/free

*Discover more "92 Tips"
and "92 Affirmations" at
www.92Tips.com*

*"Never forget that the way
you treat others will
always rebound back on
you at some point, whether
you realize it or not."*

Printed in Great Britain
by Amazon.co.uk, Ltd.,
Marston Gate.